Raising a Puppy Training Book
Easy Step by Step
Care Guide
by
Brian Mahoney

TABLE OF CONTENTS

INTRODUCTION

CHAPTER 1: Popular Dog Breeds

CHAPTER 2: Secrets to Selecting the Right Dog

CHAPTER 3: Proper Food & Nutrition for Your Dog

CHAPTER 4: Quick & Easy House Training

CHAPTER 5: Essential Dog Training Commands Part I

CHAPTER 6: Essential Dog Training Commands Part II

CHAPTER 7: Expert Social & Behavioral Training

CHAPTER 8: Puppy Loving Health Care

CONCLUSION

Introduction

Introduction

I want to thank you and congratulate you for your purchase of "The Puppy Raising Training Book".

Choosing, training, and raising a puppy is not as easy as you might think. It is especially true if it's your first time to own and raise a dog. Even experienced dog owners often find it challenging to raise and train a puppy. More so, if you have never owned a dog yourself.

Comprehensive and easy to use, this book contains all the information you need on how to choose, acquire, raise, and train a happy and healthy puppy. I wrote this intending to make it the ultimate reference book for new dog owners. I have arranged the chapters so that you get to learn as you go.

There are so many factors that you must take into account if you plan on acquiring a puppy.
For starters, you need to choose a breed that is appropriate for your lifestyle.

You need to consider the nutritional needs of the dog. You will also likely have to get the services of a veterinarian.

It would help if you also worked on the basic training and socialization needs of the pup.
And, of course, you have to think about the primary health care every dog needs.

Introduction

Bringing a new puppy home can be both exciting and overwhelming. And raising a puppy to be a behaved and healthy adult dog is a process. It takes time. It comes with a lot of difficulties and challenges, especially during the first few months.
Puppies have to learn how to do everything, and you are the one who has to teach them how to do it. As I said, it's a lot of work, but it's worth it because if you do things right, you will have a well-trained, healthy, behaved, and balanced dog that will be a source of happiness and comfort for you and your family.

Patience is a virtue you need if you want to raise a puppy. Many new dog owners don't realize how much love, time, and patience it takes to take care of a puppy. Taking care of a puppy is like taking care of a baby. You need to feed it, clean it, watch over it, and train it. All of these can be overwhelming.

A puppy's curiosity and energy can sometimes be challenging to handle. But you should not worry that much. The tasks get easier as the puppy grows older and as you get used to the routines. Just look at it as a learning process for both of you and your puppy. Another vital thing you should understand about puppies and dogs, in general, is that they are brilliant. You should not underestimate their ability to learn from and be trained by you. The speed of their learning process depends on how much time and effort you put into the endeavor.

Introduction

Using my personal experience with dogs from a young age and cutting-edge research from respected scientific journals, I will give you the information and confidence you need to establish and maintain positive expectations with your puppy. My association with family pets has improved my own life, and I want each dog and dog family to experience that same joy. It breaks my heart to see previously adored puppies left outside all day or dropped off at the local pound because the owners do not know how to train their dog.

Training a puppy is a relatively simple process that requires more time and patience than sophistication. Even if you have never trained a dog before, you can achieve success by following the suggestions in this book. Training your dog has never been simpler! I wish you the best of luck on your dog training journey. Enjoy the read!

Disclaimer Notice

This book was written as a guide and for information, educational and entertainment purposes only. No warranties of any kind are expressed or implied.

Readers acknowledge that the author is not engaging in the rendering of legal, financial, medical or professional advice, and the information in this book is not meant to take the place of any professional advice. If advice is needed in any of these fields, you are advised to seek the services of a professional.

While the author has attempted to make the information in this book as accurate as possible, no guarantee is given as to the accuracy or currency of any individual item. Laws and procedures related to business, health and well being are constantly changing.

Therefore, in no event shall the author of this book be liable for any special, indirect, or consequential damages or any damages whatsoever in connection with the use of the information herein provided.

All Rights Reserved

No part of this book may be used or reproduced in any manner whatsoever without the written permission of the author.

Copyright © 2021 MahoneyProducts
All rights reserved.

DEDICATION

**This book is dedicated to my Father
Ulester Mahoney Sr.**

ACKNOWLEDGMENTS

I WOULD LIKE TO ACKNOWLEDGE ALL THE HARD WORK OF THE MEN AND WOMEN OF THE UNITED STATES MILITARY, WHO RISK THEIR LIVES ON A DAILY BASIS, TO MAKE THE WORLD A SAFER PLACE.

CHAPTER 1: Popular Dog Breeds

Popular Dog Breeds

Choosing the right breed of dog is like shopping at a supermarket. You have dozens of options to choose from. There are various factors you need to consider to ensure that you pick the proper breed of dog. The breed you choose largely depends on who is going to spend the most time with the dog. You also take into account the people who will be in constant contact with the dog. Are there babies or children in your home? It means that you have to look for a breed that's particularly friendly and safe for babies and small children.

When choosing a dog or puppy, you have to identify the one that suits your situation. As a pet, you want a dog that has a pleasant temper and can relate well with your kids and family. The most popular dog breeds are:

Popular Dog Breeds

Labrador Retrievers

Labradors Retrievers are strong swimmers and family-oriented dogs. On the other hand, as most Labrador owners refer to them, Labs have a short coat that does not need much grooming. Their coats come in three primary colors: black, chocolate, and yellow. They are also medium-sized and can be trained to retrieve prey. Recently, they have also been used to sniff out bombs and drugs. The Labrador Retriever is an intelligent dog, eager to please their owners in any way possible. This dog is ideal for households that do not have experience raising dogs but are active and committed enough to put in the time to train and exercise their new pup.

Popular Dog Breeds

German Shepherd

Known for their handsome looks and intelligence, German Shepherds rank high among the preferred dogs trained for military missions. The German Shepherd has a double coat that needs to be groomed regularly. This large-breed dog needs regular exercise and training. Otherwise, his tendency to assume the position as the head of the pack will undoubtedly lead to trouble and fear among household members. The German Shepherd, when appropriately trained, will make any household feel safe and secure. The loyalty of this breed is known worldwide, and the breed's intelligence makes it a welcome challenge for more experienced dog owners.

Popular Dog Breeds

Golden Retrievers

Golden Retrievers are known for their double coats that range in color from red gold to light brown. They are medium-sized dogs that love to run, swim, and retrieve shot fowl for their masters. Golden Retrievers are among the most loved breeds of dogs because of their loyalty and friendliness. They are perfect for small families or households with young children. Their patience and goofiness mean that you won't have to constantly worry when you leave your kids alone with a Golden Retriever.

Popular Dog Breeds

French Bulldogs

The French Bulldog is well-loved for its active and intelligent nature. They have tiny legs that make running around a chore only too happy to do. Their short, low-maintenance coats come in black, brindle, fawn, white, liver, and tan. Their tiny bodies pack a lot of energy, and their bright eyes bespeak the playfulness that has made this breed a favorite among young couples, families, and even lone adults.

Popular Dog Breeds

Bulldog

Because of its gentle and protective nature, the bulldog is one of the most popular family pets in the world. They are well-known for developing long-lasting bonds with their owners.

Popular Dog Breeds

Beagles

Beagles are not as large as German Shepherds but are not as small as French Bulldogs either. Their convenient size and sturdy build make them great playmates for children. They are also natural hunting dogs, and they are known to work as hard as they can when they are on the trail of fresh prey. Beagles are short-haired dogs, usually sporting tri-colored coats. While they may be happy with families, they are also known for their stubbornness and selective deafness. The Beagle would fit right in with families or individuals with open areas for play and lots of time for training.

Popular Dog Breeds

Poodles

If there is one thing that can be said about the Poodle, this breed is brilliant aside from its attractive physical looks. Poodles often take the cake when it comes to dog obedience competitions because they learn quickly and are eager to please. Poodles possess a regal and aloof air, but they are affectionate and loyal to their families. Poodles come in three sizes: toy, miniature, and standard. Their coats, while wiry and dense, do not shed. It makes Poodles a perfect fit for families or individuals with allergies to fur or dander.

Popular Dog Breeds

Rottweilers

The Rottweiler is a misunderstood breed. Often, people think of this breed as highly aggressive and untrainable. However, the Rottweiler has proven to be one of the most affectionate and loyal breeds in the canine world. Rotties' key physical traits include their heavy, barrel-type body, dark coat, powerful jaws, and strong legs. Because they were initially bred to herd cattle around farmlands, this breed needs a strong leader and a consistent source of exercise. The Rottweiler is perfect for households who have had experience with dogs before and have the patience to train this affectionate breed to the best of its abilities.

Popular Dog Breeds

German Shorthaired Pointers

German Shorthaired Pointers are affectionate and obedient! They are friendly and very enthusiastic, even boisterous at times. A trained Pointer can be very loving and versatile! A trained German Shorthaired Pointer becomes very independent, up to the point you no longer need to worry about what he's doing all the time. Coupled with their natural willing behavior and bold attitude, you'll have a disciplined home guardian! On top of that, they're excellent companions as well.

Popular Dog Breeds

Yorkshire Terriers

This is a great starter dog; the breed is the perfect choice for those looking for a little lap dog. Even though this dog is small, owners must be meticulous about the hygiene demanded by this breed. Yorkshire Terriers have hair that never stops growing, so they need religious brush care and regular trimming. More so, you may have to plan for groomer visits to keep that Yorkie in good dermal condition.

So, if you are particularly diligent about keeping things at their best and want to take on a new, not-so-serious challenge, this breed may be the best pick for you.

Chapter 2: Secrets to Selecting the Right Dog

Selecting The Right Dog

When it comes to getting a dog, you have various options. You can get one from:

Animal shelters

Animal shelters are places where pets and other animals are either surrendered or brought in when the people who previously owned them cannot care for them. They also take animals found in the streets.

Adopting a pup from a shelter is a good idea since you might be saving him from eventually being euthanized (though some of the shelters have no-kill policies in place). The processing time and requirements for most animal shelters are fewer than those of animal rescue centers.

You should be very careful if you decide to go this route because:

* Some shelters may hurry you to get the pup home

* The history of some pups in the shelter is unknown

* Animals from shelters might be terrified; hence they might not be at their best behavior. This means that you might miss out on taking home a good pup just because he was afraid.

* Most animals in shelters are older. This means that finding a pup might be a problem.

Selecting The Right Dog

Rescue Organizations

Animal rescues are mostly private organizations that take in specific animals from homeless situations or abusive homes. Dog rescue centers take in some animals. Others are given temporary homes through an extensive network of foster families who host the animal until someone is found to adopt it. This is usually the rehabilitation and treatment period for the animal if it had behavioral or health problems, enabling them to regain their social ability.

Some animal rescue organizations focus on the age and breed of the animals, which is an excellent advantage for you as it you might find a pup of the breed of your liking.

The advantages of getting your pup from animal rescue centers are that you will:

* Get information from the foster family about the puppy you are interested in

* Get more involved and exposed to the puppy before adopting him due to the process involved

* Get a healthy puppy who has been neutered, spayed and vaccinated and, in some cases, trained

The main downside to getting a pup from animal shelters includes the lengthy procedure involved.

Selecting The Right Dog

Scheduling visits with the puppy of your choice can also be an issue because the animals are kept with foster families who might not always be available. Some rescues may also require doing a home visit even after the adoption is complete to ensure the pup is doing well.

Reputable Breeders

This is the best choice to go for when you want a puppy and if you want a specific breed. However, it is essential to find an ethical and responsible breeder.

You will need to do a lot of research to find one in your area because many breeders are in the business of purely making a good profit and hence go for unethical practices (puppy farming – discussed later).

To obtain information about responsible breeders in your area, you can ask other dog owners or your vet. You can also try searching the American Kennel Club Website to get a list of responsible breeders in your area.

An ethical and responsible breeder will:

* Be more than willing to show you around the breeding premises or introduce you to the pup's parents.

* Be able to answer as many questions as you can ask comfortably about the pup's care and background and the breeding practices they follow.

Selecting The Right Dog

* Be knowledgeable about the specific breeds they have on their premises.

* Be able to provide you with a contract and a health guarantee and have proper documentation of veterinary care, including medical history and vaccines.

* Not have puppies for sale all year round. They may even keep a waiting list.

* A responsible breeder may also ask about you and your family's lifestyle and why you want the pup of your choice, and how you will train and take care of it.

* Will not pressure you to take the pup.

Places you should avoid getting your puppy from

Just as there are many places that you can get your puppy from, there are also other places that you should avoid because most of these places get their puppies from puppy mills/ puppy farms.

So, what is a puppy mill?

Puppy mills are large-scale and business-oriented breeding facilities for dogs. They usually have one main goal: to generate money through breeding and selling as many puppies as possible. The dogs are usually kept in very inhumane conditions – in cages for all their lives.

Selecting The Right Dog

They are bred multiple times without regard for careful breeding or proper care. Other conditions in puppy mills include:

* Poor sanitation, which leads to parasite infestations and diseases

* Small cages stacked on top of one another that do not have ample ventilation

* Forced breeding of the female dogs allowing short periods of recovery between litters

Separation of puppies from their mothers when they are too young. This might lead to the development of behavioral problems (fear and anxiety) and health issues (such as kennel cough and pneumonia) as the pup grows.

In addition to causing harm to the dogs, puppy mills are indifferent to the type of breeds they produce because of a lack of regard to genetic quality. This may lead to puppy breeds prone to hereditary and congenital conditions such as respiratory disorders and heart disease.

Most of the pups from puppy mills are sold through:

Pet stores

Purchasing your dog from a pet store is not recommended because most of the dogs from pet stores come from puppy mills, which you do not want to support.

Selecting The Right Dog

If you want a pure-bred pup and do not want to go through a rescue group, then it is preferable to get a puppy from a breeder instead.

Online classifieds

The first place most beginners start their search for a puppy is on the internet. Be careful as it can lead you along the wrong path because the largest market for puppy mills and backyard breeders is online sales.

Some of the pups you find here may have a lot of behavioral problems and health issues. Further, most of the dogs sold online are unwanted and may even be stolen. There is a wide range of possibilities that make finding a healthy pup online near impossible.

However, this does not necessarily mean that all websites sell puppies from puppy mills or stolen pups. If you want to obtain a puppy online, go to the official website of a known rescue group or shelter.

You can also go for reliable websites such as Petfinder. Once you find the puppy of your choice online, make sure you visit the facility in person to establish the conditions that they keep their pups in and the health of the pups.

Picking the Best Puppy for You

This is the moment of truth. What kind of animal will you choose? There are several essential things to remember when picking a new puppy, especially if the puppy is part of a large litter.

Selecting The Right Dog

First, break down the decision process into two stages. The first stage is observing the puppy with the rest of the littermates. It can tell you a lot about the puppy's personality.

The second part of the process involves you and the puppy alone together. This is also very revealing if you know what you are looking for.

There are three things to remember when evaluating puppies before choosing: position in the pack, sociability with humans, and intelligence. These three things are vital in helping to establish the dog you should choose.

Watching how a puppy interacts with other dogs, especially its littermates, can tell you a lot. Judging a puppy's position in the pack is extremely important. Is it the dominant puppy? Is it the weakling? These personality extremes are best for novice dog owners to avoid.

Why? As appealing as their rambunctiousness may seem, dominant puppies usually turn out to be dominant dogs that can be difficult to control and train. They may bully their new "littermates," who will be your kids and your kids' friends.

Many people are moved by watching the litter's weakling puppy. They want to rescue it from the rest of the pack and nurse it because they feel sorry for it. These dogs present their problems. They usually lack confidence, both in the canine and the human world.

Selecting The Right Dog

It can lead to trainability problems and problems with human interaction later on. Is either of these two dogs ever going to find a home? Yes. A more experienced person can better understand these puppies' needs.

For newcomers to dog ownership, a more stable-tempered, middle-of-the-road pup is best. Such a pup is neither pushed around too easily nor overly dominant with its littermates or mother.

The next thing to judge is how the puppy responds to your presence. You probably shouldn't go for the first one who comes rushing at you. Neither do you want the one who won't come at all. You want one of middling temperament. A follower? That is a good dog. You certainly don't want your dog to be a leader. That's your position.

A little pup too busy to come over to you or too afraid to come over to you probably isn't a suitable pet. While socialization with dogs is important, socialization with people is also key since your puppy will be living night and day with you and your family, not his.

Remember that you are a giant to a young puppy even if you weigh less than 100 pounds. Just the sheer size of you can be scary to them. The best way to petition a little puppy to approach you is to bend on one knee and place your hand lower than its head.

Selecting The Right Dog

The idea is to offer something that is not so intimidating. You're trying to get an honest read of the dog's personality. You are not trying to scare the heck out of it.

Chapter Summary

As you can see, there are plenty of dog breeds, each with their own unique personalities and characteristics. For a successful lifetime relationship, it is important to start with a dog that best matches your personality and lifestyle.

Don't be afraid to ask questions from a trusted breeder, an experienced rescue person, or even a store owner. Take your time. Find the right Puppy for you and your family for years of happy companionship.

Chapter 3: Proper Food & Nutrition For Your Dog

Food & Nutrition

Nutrition is vital for your growing puppy, and the mass of dog food options on the market can be overwhelming. This chapter will cover the basics of what your puppy needs to grow healthy and strong while also helping you choose feeding options that fit your lifestyle.

What to Feed Your Puppy

There are a few different ways to approach feeding your puppy, and each has its advantages and disadvantages. This section will guide you through your decision-making process, helping you choose the best option for your puppy and you. It's crucial to select a pet food based on your puppy's age and growth phase, keeping any medical concerns in mind. Please consult with your veterinarian about your food selection to ensure it meets your puppy's needs.

Dry Kibble

Kibble is the most common choice for feeding puppies and adult dogs. It's low-cost, has a long shelf life, and doesn't require any special storage. It also has the added benefit of massaging your puppy's gums and teeth to a degree, contributing to improved oral health. There are many options available on the market, but not all are equally appropriate for your puppy.

When choosing a kibble brand, check first for an AAFCO certification label on the bag. It indicates that the product has undergone testing and feeding trials by the Association of American Feed Control Officials and has been deemed balanced and appropriate for use.

Food & Nutrition

Next, consider the ingredient list on the back of the bag. Dogs, unlike cats, are not strict carnivores. Plant-based ingredients like grains, fruits, and vegetables are not just dietary fillers; they contain important vitamins, minerals, and fiber that contribute to your puppy's overall health and development. That said, a protein should be one of the first three ingredients listed.

You will also want to research the manufacturer and company to ensure you're buying a reputable brand with good quality-control measures. Veterinary-exclusive brands, such as Medi-Cal, Hill's, or Science Diet, are among my top brand recommendations for their rigorous research, feeding trials, and quality-control practices, but plenty of other great options are out there.

Wet Food

Wet or canned food often has the same ingredients as kibble but in different ratios. For example, wet food is, of course, much higher in water than kibble. Canned food is packaged in durable containers and generally has a long shelf life, but once it's opened, it must be refrigerated and fed to your puppy within a few days, or it'll go bad. Wet food is often more palatable to dogs, so it may be a better choice for a picky eater. However, it's also more expensive than kibble. If you're looking to both save money and add flavor, try mixing a few tablespoons of yummy wet food in with your dog's kibble at each meal instead of feeding them wet food alone.

Food & Nutrition

Raw Food

Although it may be an option to look into when your dog is older, raw diets are not recommended for puppies. They need to get enough calcium and phosphorus as they grow, and if the raw diet is not appropriately balanced, it can result in bone deformities and growth issues.

There are also some significant health risks to consider. There's no guarantee that these products are free of dangerous pathogens, such as *Salmonella* or *E. coli*, which can cause vomiting, diarrhea, fevers, and occasionally death for dogs. If you or your kids accidentally ingest bacteria like these when preparing and feeding raw meals, when your puppy licks you, or even when scooping your puppy's poop, you could suffer the same consequences.

Homemade Food

Some owners choose to make their puppy food at home, which can theoretically be fine as long as you ensure that the diet is nutritionally balanced and appropriate for your dog's life stage. The problem is that this is very difficult to do. A team of researchers at UC Davis found that of the 200 homemade dog food recipes they tested, 95 percent lacked "at least one essential nutrient," and over 83 percent had "multiple nutrient deficiencies."

Even recipes by veterinarians sometimes fell short. If you choose to take this route, use recipes created by veterinary *nutritionists*, and don't experiment or stray from the recipe.

Food & Nutrition

It's also recommended to consult with and have your puppy's diet evaluated by a veterinary nutritionist. You'll need a food scale to ensure you're using the proper ratios of ingredients and feeding appropriate amounts to your puppy. And remember, you'll have to adjust the recipe as your puppy grows!

Additionally, make sure you cook meat thoroughly to destroy potential pathogens that can make your pet ill.

How Much and How Often to Feed

Now that you know what to do when it comes to picking out a type of dog food, you're probably wondering how much food you should be feeding your puppy as well as how often you should be feeding them. Puppies, being baby dogs, are similar to baby humans in that they should eat multiple small meals per day as opposed to a few large meals. Also, similar to baby food, these meals should be formulated with their nutritional needs in mind.

Generally, your puppy will finish their meal as it's put down, but if not, you should not leave their food down for more than 10 to 20 minutes. It would be best if you also were sure to feed your puppy these meals in consistent portions and at consistent times to prevent picky eating habits.

When making decisions about how much to feed your puppy, the most important thing to pay attention to is how your puppy looks physically. In other words, pay more attention to the pup than the food bowl.

Food & Nutrition

This is because each puppy has a different body build, metabolism, and nutritional needs. Most food brands will provide you with a baseline amount to feed your puppy based on their age and weight. You may continue to assess how your dog does with the amount of food you give them from there. If you see your dog begin to gain weight and become rounder than their body type suggests, you may begin to lessen their food intake.

Another sign that you may want to lessen the amount of food you give your puppy is continuously leaving food in the bowl or skipping meals. If you see your dog begin to lose weight and become too narrow for its body type, you may want to increase your puppy's food intake. Another factor you may want to consider is whether or not you are using treats during training. If so, be sure to adjust your puppy's food intake as necessary. To give you a clearer indication of where your puppy should be throughout the beginning of its stage of life, we'll go through a puppy's first year feeding schedule below.

Six to twelve weeks old: At six to twelve weeks old, your puppy should undoubtedly be eating puppy food still as adult dog food will not have the necessary nutrients that your puppy needs for proper growth. During this stage of life, your puppy should be eating about four times a day. A small breed puppy should be eating dry food without moisture by about twelve to thirteen weeks, while a large breed puppy should be eating dry food by about nine to ten weeks.

Food & Nutrition

Three to six months old: Towards about twelve weeks old, your puppy should begin to lose its baby belly and overall roundness. If you find that your puppy is still pudgy at this stage of life, you should continue to find them puppy-sized portions until their weight starts to even out with their body size. At this point, you should switch from feeding your pup four meals per day to three meals per day.

Six to 12 months old: By the time your puppy is six to twelve months old, you should only be feeding them about twice per day. This is around the time you will likely have your puppy neutered or spayed. Since this procedure will lower your puppy's energy level, you will be able to switch from nutrient-filled puppy food over to adult dog food afterward. Bigger breeds can be switched over to adult food at about 12 to 14 months, while smaller breeds can switch to adult food at about seven to nine months. This switch should be made with caution, though, as it is better to have your pup on puppy food for too long instead of adult food too soon.

After one year: Once your puppy is about a year old, they should generally eat about two portions of food per day. At this point, you can generally go off of recommended feeding portions that are listed on the bag of dog food that you are using.

Food & Nutrition

Maintaining an eye on your dog's weight and checking it with your vet now and again will ensure that they are getting the proper amount of food and nutrition as they continue through life.

All-Important Water

No discussion of what to feed a dog is complete without mentioning water. It is a nutrient as essential to dogs as it is to other living things. Dogs can go longer without food than they can without water. To stay hydrated and cool off, dogs need a constant supply of fresh, clean, cool water.

It's necessary to leave out a clean bowl of water at all times for your puppy or adult dog. Never regulate the water supply. Dogs can't tell you when they are thirsty, so you must leave water for them at all times. When they're thirsty, they will drink. Change the water in your dog's bowl a few times a day, and clean the bowl thoroughly once a day. Attention to the water bowl may also alert you to any changes in how much — or little — your dog is drinking, which can be an indication of a severe medical condition.

Don't let your dog drink out of the toilet. This is not a substitute for a water bowl, and in fact, could be contaminated with bacteria and residue from the toxic cleaning products that could seriously harm your dog.

Food & Nutrition

Supplements

There are many nutritional supplements on the market for dogs, and it can be confusing to know what your dog needs. Common supplements that address specific medical conditions include joint supplements such as glucosamine for adult or senior dogs and fish oils or omega-3 fatty acids to support dry, dull, or itchy skin.

If you are feeding your puppy an appropriate and nutritionally balanced diet, there is usually no need for supplements. Please consult with your vet before adding one to your puppy's diet to ensure it's safe and effective. You might need pharmaceuticals to address a medical concern adequately, but supplements can often support the treatment or help prevent the problem from reoccurring. And make sure you follow your vet's or the product's guidelines and use the correct dose for your puppy's age and weight.

Treats

Treats are a great way to show affection to dogs, praise them for a job well done, or train them on new skills and behaviors. While giving treats to your dog is okay—and even encouraged in many scenarios—like all good things, it should be done in moderation. Treats are formulated to be tasty and valuable, not wholesome and nutritionally balanced. They shouldn't make up the bulk of your dog's daily caloric intake, and overfeeding can result in excessive weight gain.

Food & Nutrition

Warning! Not Safe for Puppies!

Puppies and even dogs can get sick if they overeat their puppy chow or dog food. They can also become prone to diarrhoea if you give them too many treats and table scraps. There are also specific kinds of food that your puppy should stay away from.

Chocolates

These tasty pick-me-ups are not suitable for puppies and dogs because of their caffeine and theobromine content. More than ten ounces of chocolate can make your pup suffer from diarrhoea, vomiting, and shaking.

Xylitol

Xylitol is a substance that is often used as a substitute for sugar. It can be found in alcohol, berries, mushrooms, and some other fruits. Too much xylitol can stimulate a release of insulin that may prove to be fatal for your pup.

Alcohol

Do not attempt to share alcohol with your pup or dog. Most alcohol products contain ingredients that are toxic to our canine friends. These ingredients include grapes, grape seeds, and yeast. If your pup ingests alcohol, it may exhibit signs of confusion, dizziness, or lack of motor control.

Onions and Garlic

Onions and garlic, as members of the Allium family, contain the toxic substance N-propyl disulfide. This substance can lead to anemia and digestive problems for your pup.

Food & Nutrition

Dairy Products

Aside from their mom's milk, your pup or dog should not be given access to dairy products such as cow's or goat's milk. While cheese can be given as rare treats, they should not constitute a large part of your pup's meals. These dairy products can easily upset your pup's stomach and lead to diarrhoea or vomiting.

Should your puppy or dog ingest any of the five types of food listed above, it is best to contact your vet for help. Then, remember to keep these types of food away from your pup to prevent any future incidents.

Chapter Summary

There are plenty of options out there, when it comes to feeding your dog. Take the time to do the proper research and that will help to reduce the chances of serious health issues down the road.

Spending more now, for the best nutrition, is an investment for a lifetime of health and happiness for you and your dog.

Chapter 4: Quick & Easy House Training

Quick & Easy House Training

The first thing every new owner should know before bringing a puppy into the house is how to teach him where to relieve himself. The good news is that all puppies can be house trained. The bad news is that a puppy rarely becomes house trained by just letting him out several times a day. This comprehensive house training plan requires dedication — but it's simple and foolproof.

The Essentials of house training

This is your to-do list to get started. There are only a few items on it, so it's not too difficult. If you can keep to it, you will be amazed at how well house-training goes. If you get off track, resolve to get back on as quickly as possible. You can do it!

1. Confine your puppy to his crate when you can't watch him so he won't relieve himself where he's not supposed to or while you are not looking (if you prefer, use a baby gate to confine him to the kitchen or laundry room while you can't watch him).
2. Supervise your puppy when he is out of his crate.
3. Feed him a high-quality diet at scheduled times and limit treats.
4. Take him to his potty spot as soon as you return home, soon after meals, and when he wakes up from a nap.
5. Teach him to eliminate on command by saying Go potty, Good puppy! in an excited voice while he's doing his business.

Quick & Easy House Training

6. Clean up his accidents immediately (remove debris or moisture, then treat with neutralizer and cleaner).

7. Never correct him after the fact.

Make arrangements for when you are away

If you, as of now, have a pup and should be away for extensive periods, you will need to:

• Arrange for somebody, like a mindful neighbor or an expert pet sitter, to take them for release breaks.

• Alternatively, train them to dispose of in a particular spot inside. Know, in any case, that doing this can drag out the interaction of house training.

The Importance of Schedules

Most puppies leave their litter to enter their new home at about two months of age. At this age, the pups eat and drink a lot and have limited ability to control their elimination and no comprehension that might be important.

Feeding and potty times should be adjusted to help puppy reach his potential in the house training department as quickly as possible. At two to four months of age, most pups need to relieve themselves after waking up, eating, playing, sleeping and drinking — perhaps as often as every thirty to forty-five minutes, depending on the type and amount of activity.

At four months, the puppy may be developed like an adult internally, but expect him to behave like a puppy.

Quick & Easy House Training

To housetrain effectively, you need to establish a schedule that works for your family and will help your puppy learn the rules quickly. You will be amazed at how quickly your puppy learns if you stick to a schedule with fixed times for eating, sleeping, and exercising.

Puppies can dehydrate very easily and very quickly. It is extremely important that you give your puppy ample access to water. Restricting your puppy's water as a means of potty training should only be done as a last resort and only after consulting with your puppy's veterinarian.

Potty training will go differently depending on a few different aspects. First, how old is your pup? Experts recommend that house training begins between 12 and 16 weeks old because, at this age, your pup will learn how to control their bowel and bladder. If your dog is older, training could take longer. Second, where did you get your dog from? If your dog came from the pound or rescue, it is less likely that they will be potty trained. Good breeders will take the time to teach basic concepts like potty training to a litter. That way, the dogs will understand the concept and will be able to learn faster in your home.

Old Fashioned Training

Some people like to stick with the old-fashioned way of making their pup go outside. If you want to make this a solid occurrence, you will need to take the time to make a schedule. An excellent guide to follow when it comes to puppies is that their age in months corresponds to the number of hours they can hold their bladder.

Quick & Easy House Training

As for creating the schedule, this should be based on your life and your puppy's habits. If your puppy is still young and has a small bladder, try taking them out:

* In the morning
* After playing
* After chewing on a toy
* After drinking
* After eating
* After time in their crate
* Last thing at night

Of course, most of us will be unable to keep this type of schedule up, but it is necessary to have your dog being potty trained. If you are at work, try hiring a dog walker or bringing your pup to work with you. The quicker you get the idea of potty time through your dog's head, the sooner they will learn.

Once your schedule is determined, try picking a bathroom spot outside that you consider acceptable for your dog. When you begin potty training your pup, it is always suggested to keep them on a leash.

Once you approach the selected potty spot, try using words like "go potty" to help teach your pup. As a reward, you can try giving them a treat once they go to the bathroom or allow some play time once the deed is done. Sometimes, praising your pup is enough, but this should be done once you are back inside the house.

Quick & Easy House Training

This way, your dog can connect the event to the praise and try to do it again. Also, be aware that you should not reward your puppy too quickly. It is possible to distract your dog mid-bathroom, and they will forget to finish. If this happens, they could finish inside the house. Try to avoid giving a reward too quickly, and the lesson should be smooth sailing ahead.

Your pup should have not only a bathroom schedule but also a set feeding schedule. The feeding schedule will differ depending on the age of your dog. If they are still puppies, your dog should be fed three or four times per day. Try to make feeding time around the same time to take them out directly after and create an ideal schedule for food and bathroom.

It is also suggested to try picking up your pup's water dish two or three hours before bedtime. This way, they will be less likely to wake you up in the middle of the night because their bladder is full. An average puppy can sleep for seven hours without having to use the bathroom. However, if a pup does wake you up, try not to discourage them, no matter how annoyed you may be. Take your dog out to do their business and immediately bring them back in. It would be best if you left no time for play time as this may mess up your ideal schedule.

When training your dog, you need to expect your pup to make mistakes. Training will always have a few hiccups, and you need to deal with them mildly. Luckily, there are a few steps you can take to discourage your dog without making them fearful.

Quick & Easy House Training

Catch Them: If you catch your puppy in the act, you should clap loudly so that your dog realizes that what they are doing is wrong. Once they are stopped, bring your dog outside for them to finish. Once they are done, be sure to praise them for going outside.

Avoid Aftermath Punishment: If you come home and scold your pup for making a mess inside, you will confuse them.

As we said before, your dog cannot make connections once time has passed. Instead, clean up the accident with no punishment and fix the problem during the next bathroom lesson. There is an old punishment where rubbing your pup's nose in the mess will fix the problem. It is wrong. As a pet parent, you should always avoid getting aggressive toward your dog as it may backfire and cause distrust for you.

Cleaning Up: When your dog makes a mess in the house, you need to clean it up as thoroughly as possible. Often, dogs will search for their scent to go to the bathroom in the exact location. It is suggested you use an enzymatic cleanser than then an ammonia-based one to help minimize the odor.

Paper Training and Puppy Pads

For those who live in a city, going outside may not always be convenient, especially if you live in a high-rise building where it would take some time to get outside. Or, for those of you who have small dogs, the winter can be a struggle for bathroom time.

Quick & Easy House Training

Losing your small dog out in the piles of snow is not always ideal. This is where puppy pads can come in handy.

One of the most critical factors of puppy pad training is keeping an eye on your dog. If your dog has the chance to sneak away, they could have an accident on your floor without you realizing. If you are unable always to watch your dog, a crate is suggested. In the next section, we will be talking all about crate training.

Next, you will want to be sure that your potty pad is in a place that is both accessible for your dog and in a location you plan on keeping the pad. At all costs, you will want to avoid moving the pad while your puppy is learning.

If you plan on going outside, bring the pad outside with you so that your dog will recognize the papers as an appropriate place to relieve themselves. While training a puppy, it is suggested to bring your pup to the pad about 5 minutes before you think they need to eliminate. This way, it will be easier to make the connection. Be sure to say 'Go potty" or whichever phrase you choose to use each time.

When your pup does use the potty pad, always praise them and give them a treat. Remember: if your dog does have an accident inside without your knowledge, do not punish them. They will not connect why they are being punished and may become fearful of you. Instead, clean the mess up and try again.

Quick & Easy House Training

Though the training takes time, it will be convenient to live in the city and not worry about taking your pup out to do their business.

Crate Training

Much like humans, dogs hate a soiled rug as much as you do. They would much rather live in a clean home. It is why crate training could be a good option for potty training. The tool is excellent for potty and travel, vet visits, and safety purposes.

First things first, you should make sure that your crate is large enough for your puppy. The box should be large enough for your pup to lie down, stand, and turn around in. However, if the crate is too big, there is a chance that your dog could use one corner as the bathroom and still lay in the same crate. You want to discourage this. While training, you will want to be able to stay home with your dog to train them. When your pup needs to go to the bathroom, they will wine, and that is when you can let the dog out to go to the bathroom.

If you plan on crate training, be sure that someone will be home to give your pup a break from the kennel. Bad habits can form if you allow your pup to use his crate as the bathroom. Instead, look for your dog's signs that he needs to use the bathroom. These can range from: barking, circling, sniffing, scratching, or whining. If your dog does any of these, be sure to take her out right away. Once your pup has finished her business, remember to reward her. Either way, she will learn where she can and cannot relieve herself.

Quick & Easy House Training

Bathroom training is essential when you get a dog. The sooner you train your pup to use the bathroom how you want, the less time you will spend cleaning up after them. If you have to be away from home for more than four or five hours a day, a puppy may not be the best fit for your life.

puppies require a lot of time and effort. Instead, you should consider an older dog who can hold their bladder until you return. Either way, make sure your dog knows where they need to go. That way, as you both grow older, it will not be an issue you need to continue working on.

How to Handle Accidents

No matter how careful you are, occasionally, inappropriate elimination happens. If your puppy has an accident, do the following:

Never correct the puppy after the fact. Do scold yourself by saying, "How could I have let that happen?"

If you catch him in the act, startle him by saying "Ach" loudly or picking him up in midstream and carrying him outside to stop him.

Until your puppy is perfectly potty trained, remember:

1. Puppies who can hold it for long periods while they are in their cage or at night are not necessarily well on their way to being housebroken.

Quick & Easy House Training

2. Don't judge his capacity and trustworthiness by his behavior while crated. Metabolism slows down with inactivity, so even an untrained puppy may not soil for up to twelve hours when he's crated. Puppies aren't trained until they understand it's okay to move about, explore, and go potty outdoors, but must hold it as they move about and explore indoors.

3. Puppies enjoy playing, observing, and investigating and often forget about going potty when they are left alone outdoors. Don't let your puppy out without supervision and assume that he did his business. Even if your puppy has just spent a lot of time outdoors, he may mess soon after he comes back inside.

4. Puppies often indicate when they want to go outdoors and play, instead of when they need to potty. Don't rely on or encourage him to tell you he wants to go out. Many puppies will indicate frequently and always eliminate when taken to the potty area. This causes bladder and bowel capacity and control to be underdeveloped. So, if he is used to going out on demand to go potty, he may have to relieve himself immediately whether you are available or not.

Quick & Easy House Training

Chapter Summary

There is probably nothing more frustrating than having a dog that is not properly housebroken. No one wants to come home from a long day at the office to find that the dog has urinated or defecated anywhere in the house.

When it comes to puppy training it is likely that house training is the least pleasant of all tasks that an owner will undertake, but it must be done with patience, love, and consideration.

Chapter 5: Essential Dog Training Commands Part 1

Dog Training Commands Part I

The principles of obedience training are elementary to grasp, and you can get started with your pet whenever you wish. Of course, it's a good idea to start simple and focus on mastering a few basic commands that every good dog should know. It will help get you used to how your dog thinks and responds to different rewards and cues. You will also quickly get a feel for how fast the puppy learns and what sort of pace you should maintain.

It would help if you also remember that neither you nor your dog is robots. Try and approach the whole thing in a casual, natural manner without worrying too much about the results. You are working with a puppy; after all, you can treat your training sessions as a fun hobby and a way to play with your pet. It's important not to bring stress into these sessions because you don't want your puppy learning to associate obedience training with something stressful or something that she is afraid of.

Positive Training

"Positive training," or "positive-reinforcement training," uses rewards and consequences to train a dog—*not* punishment. In this context, a consequence might be preventing your puppy's access to a person or reward (such as treats), but it is never painful, frightening, or intimidating. Positive training doesn't use "aversive techniques," such as physical reprimands or yelling, focusing instead on the animal's wellbeing.

Dog Training Commands Part I

Positive training is the preferred choice; it is respectful for both you and your puppy and focuses on relationship building through communication, clear criteria, rewards, and consequences.

The puppy is free to learn through mistakes, as they don't have to fear punishment for guessing wrong. It results in a more engaged dog in their training and openly offers behaviors to you, which you can then reward if you approve or ignore if you don't!

Name Recognition

Before you start basic obedience training, you must teach your puppy her name. Your puppy's name should always engage a positive reaction from you. For this reason, you must not discipline your puppy after saying her name.

The best way to teach pup's name is to use it frequently and positively. Always use an excited tone when you say your puppy's name. You may find that your pup associates this with come. You could choose to teach pup's name as an alternative to come, but other people find it is helpful to keep the commands separate. It will eventually teach your puppy to look at you when you say her name.

"Come" command

For how banal and straightforward this command is, you would be forgiven for forgetting its great importance. Some people would probably not even call this a command since you will do it a hundred times every day.

Dog Training Commands Part I

In the simplest terms, this essential first step is all about getting your dog to pay attention to you, even at the expense of whatever they are doing at that time. A well-trained dog will even drop the most delicious meal if her owner calls upon him. Such a dog is also a safe dog because her owner will never have to worry about him rushing out into the street despite being called to come back.

The first element in this exercise is to give your dog a simple, catchy name as early as possible and make sure that you stick with it. After that, all you have to do is repeat the name enough times and make sure that your dog associates it with something pleasant, and he will quickly learn that this name means, "Pay attention!" Of course, the easiest way to do this is through rewards. Quite simply, try calling your puppy, and whenever she pays attention to you and comes over, you should use a treat and/or your clicker.

You will do more-or-less the same thing when teaching your dog the recall command, which is usually tied to the cue word "come." Just keep repeating and rewarding every time your dog does what he is supposed to. In general, it's a good idea to practice this in calm, controlled conditions early on. It would be ideal to have a quiet and private room for these training sessions because puppies can easily get overwhelmed by too many stimuli and lose focus. It is also a good idea to use gestures, body language, and friendly tones when trying to get your puppy to come over.

Dog Training Commands Part I

It is certainly one of the easiest things to teach your dog, and it generally comes naturally, especially when you start working with a small puppy. The more times the puppy comes over to you and gets a reward for it, the more cemented this habit will become in the dog's memory when he gets older.

"Sit" command

Teaching your dog to sit is a great first step in obedience training. This command will likely be relatively easy for your dog to learn, so it will give him a nice boost of confidence to get started. It will also help you start to get comfortable training your pup!

This command is easy to practice anywhere; all you need are some tasty treats. The technique here is a simple one. Hold a tasty treat in your hand and bring it close to your dog's nose. Once he's smelled the delicious treat you're hiding, slowly bring your hand up over your dog's head so her hindquarters move toward the floor. The moment he's seated, say "sit" and give him the treat.

Continue practicing this sequence of steps a few times throughout the day. Once it's automatic, you can start having your dog sit before mealtimes or going outside. Eventually, "sit" will be so comfortable and routine, you'll be able to say "sit," and your pup will promptly sit down by your side.

Dog Training Commands Part I

"Down" command

It's important to teach your dog to sit first, as they must learn that before moving on lying down. You can easily build off of sitting and transition from standing to sitting to lying down. It makes it much easier for you to train your dog, and it makes it a lot easier for your dog to understand you. Teaching it "down" can help when training your dog to use its bed or crate. It can also be helpful in any situation where he needs to settle. Additionally, it's a fun trick to teach your dog, and it is also a great building block.

Once you have mastered the "sit" command, you are ready to teach your dog to lie down. First, ask your dog to sit. You may reward it for doing so. After this, take another treat and hold it up to its nose. Drag the treat down towards the floor and away from its face. The dog should naturally lie down to get the treat. Once they lay down on the floor, give it the treat and reward him. You may also click your clicker once they lie down. Add in a vocal command such as "down" or "lay down" to help it even more. Adding a hand gesture can also help it. It would be best if you used a different hand gesture from the "sit" command. You may mimic the treat going down, or you may choose a hand gesture of your own. Regardless, it would help if you stayed consistent with your hand gesture and verbal command. Otherwise, your dog can become confused by what it is that you are looking for.

Dog Training Commands Part I

"Stay" command

As you probably know, teaching your dog to stay means having him stay put on command until told to move. This command is another fairly simple and straightforward one, but it might take a bit more time for your dog to master because you will have to be pretty gradual.

The stay command consists of two cues: telling your dog to stay and another for letting him know it's okay to move. In general, the verbal cue for the former is "stay" (often combined with a hand gesture), while the release cue can be a simple "okay." Keep in mind that this command is much easier to teach if your dog has already mastered the sit and lie down commands.

The combination with sitting is a common and fairly easy approach. Get your pup to sit down and pay attention to you while keeping a few treats in your pocket. At first, you can try and do this as if your dog was a genius. Namely, after getting your dog to sit, try, and tell him to stay while also using a stop-sign hand gesture, with your palm facing the dog. After that, try to take one or two steps backward and see what the puppy does. If she stays put, you should praise and reward her. From that point on, it's just a matter of increasing the number of steps after giving the cue and before rewarding the dog until you can eventually leave the room and break visual contact while your dog still stays put.

Dog Training Commands Part I

"Heel" command

The "heel" command is an easy command to teach your puppy, especially if you take him out regularly to exercise.

This will require a lot of treats and patience on your end. You can also start this exercise with a leash to keep your puppy from straying too far.

To walk your dog correctly, make sure he knows staying beside you is better than straying too far from you. You might want to give your dog a short jog before starting this exercise to wean off the excess energy he has or to tire him out a bit.

You can use this command to make your puppy less apprehensive of sounds outside your home. Try doing this exercise while traversing a busy sidewalk. Be vigilant at this point and make sure he heels whenever he feels too curious. Stop walking if he does not listen to you.

You can also use a whistle at this point to call him back to you if he strays too far. As soon as he is near you, give the command to "heel" so he understands that this means he has to stay by your side at all times.

"No" or "stop" command

The stop or no command is the first command you should teach your pup —fortunately, dogs, especially puppies, master both (or one of) these commands easily.

Dog Training Commands Part I

When teaching this command, say the words firmly and authoritatively, but avoid hitting your dog as you do this or when it fails to comply with the command.

Whenever you see the dog doing something wrong, say 'stop' or 'no,' then pull it from whatever it was doing and repeat the word. Keep repeating the command whenever you find the dog doing something wrong until it can obey consistently.

"Watch" command

There are moments where it's beneficial to get your dog's attention. You can get your dog to pay attention to you, while it will help with training and giving commands. It can also help if you need to distract your dog from undesired behavior. Overall, it can help you communicate better with your dog if he can pay attention to you.

You will want your dog to respond to "watch," "look," or some other variation of that. Ensure that you choose a different command from others so that your dog will understand what you are asking for. It would be best if you mastered the basics before moving on this. This is because you will need to be able to get your dog's attention. It should trust you and have an understanding of how training works. Your dog should be able to take commands from you and follow them.

To teach your dog how to watch you, you will want to have it on a leash and get it to sit in front of you. Hold your dog's leash with one hand and put some treats in the other.

Dog Training Commands Part I

Your dog should develop an interest in the treats and may even begin sniffing at them. Gradually move the treats towards your face. Make eye contact with your dog. When your dog turns its glance to you instead of the treats, praise and reward it for its effort. Repeat this, adding in the command right before your dog diverts her attention to you.

To master this skill, try doing it without treats. Use a hand signal and verbal cue, rewarding your dog after it listens to you. Ease off of the hand signal and begin to use the verbal command more often. You may make a smaller path with the hand signal to ease into this. You can also try having it watch you and then taking a step away. Reward your dog for following you. You can make your movements faster, farther, and harder to follow

"Off" command

If you wish to stop your dog from constantly getting onto a chair or settee, the off command is handy. You teach it by having a treat enclosed in both hands, but for this, do keep your hands closed. Place one closed hand near to your dog's face so that the scent of the treat can be detected. The dog will not be able to get the treat because your hand is closed. He will stop trying. At this point, open your hand and offer the treat. Use the command off, repeat it several times until the dog understands and then, reward him.

Dog Training Commands Part I

"Quiet" command

This command will help you stop chronic dog barking. Keep a bag of treats with you at all times, just if you are ever in a situation when you need it to stop barking.

When it does, look at it and say 'quiet' with a treat in your hand. As soon as it stops barking, praise it, and give it the treat. If it still does not stop, show it the treat and try to get it to stop. Repeat this until the dog can stop barking after you say the command.

Chapter summary

Every dog and person benefits from learning the basic commands. You start by luring but then need to move to rewarding after the skill has been done. Once your dog knows a skill, move to intermittent rewarding by giving a food reward every second, third, or fourth time.

Chapter 6: Essential Dog Training Commands Part II

Dog Training Commands Part II

Once you've covered the basics and your dog has a decent grasp on the simple commands and the key rules around the house, you can also try and teach him some more complicated stuff or just get the things he already knows to a new, advanced level. Besides, by the time you take care of all the basics, your puppy will already be on her way toward adolescence, and she will be ready to tackle some more complicated lessons.

We'll look at a few such lessons in this chapter, and you will find that they have a range of benefits. Sometimes, these tricks and commands look cool but much more important is how they will make your life easier and your dog safer and healthier.

Leash training

Leash training is a valuable skill for both you and your puppy. Walks or traveling will be much easier once your pup is comfortable and confident walking on a leash. Help your puppy become a model pup citizen when he's out in the world by starting leash training early. We recommend using a 6-foot leash made of nylon or leather to start training. While a longer leash may tempt you, training will go more smoothly with a shorter one as there's less slack for your pup to take advantage of. While training, avoid flexible or retractable leashes. Once your dog is fully leash trained, you might decide to incorporate those into your walks. But for training purposes, these types of leashes will hinder training.

Dog Training Commands Part II

Start slow inside your house by allowing your puppy to get used to his collar and leash or leash and harness combo. Let him wear it for a few minutes during playtime and reward him with treats, so he comes to associate the leash with something he likes.

After your pup has learned the "come" command, you can start practicing walking on the leash inside. A hallway or a quiet room with few distractions would be a good place to start. With your pup wearing the leash, encourage him to take a few steps toward you by calling his name and rewarding him with treats. Slowly back up, so he has to continue walking toward you for his reward.

When you're ready to move outside, arm yourself with a bag of treats. When you first begin leash training, choose a spot your pup is already familiar with, like the backyard or somewhere close by in the neighborhood. It will keep distractions to a minimum. Practice walking with your puppy by your side so you maintain control over direction and speed. Puppies, who are curious by nature, tend to veer off the path to go exploring or have a sniff. While he's young, it's best to keep him close by, but once he's older and more confident on the leash, you can give him greater freedom to explore if you wish.

Whenever your pup is walking by your side with a loose leash, praise him lavishly and offer the occasional treat for his good behavior. Ensure you give your dog time to do his business, but try to keep a steady pace throughout the walk.

Dog Training Commands Part II

If your dog does become sidetracked by a bunch of flowers or a particularly intriguing patch of grass, avoid the urge to pull or tug his leash to get him moving. Instead, reward him for coming to you when you call him back to your side.

Speaking of pulling - this is one of the bad behaviors many dogs struggle with on walks. There's just so much to explore and catch their attention. However, constantly being jerked by your pup or feeling like he's the one walking you does not make for an enjoyable stroll around the neighborhood. It can also lead to injury in your dog.

When you find your dog repeatedly pulling on his leash, make it like a tree and stand completely still until he stops pulling. While this might make walks a little stop-and-go for a while, it will help your pup grow accustomed to walking comfortably by your side. You can also shorten the amount of slack you leave on the leash to deter pulling. Remember to keep praising and rewarding your pup for his excellent work when he walks beside you with a loose leash.

Another common problem is lunging. The walk seems to be going fine until your puppy sees a chipmunk or a neighbor he's desperate to investigate. You have two options here: either avoid the trigger or try to distract your puppy's attention with a treat. Sometimes the best option is simply to turn around and walk the other way. Other times, you might use a treat to distract your pup's attention before he has the opportunity to lunge.

Dog Training Commands Part II

Having the leash on while working on commands like 'wait,' 'leave it,' and 'take it' will make it easier for them to understand that those commands are part of long walks. Avoid taking your puppy out on a leash to anywhere that there might be strange dogs or animals, though. Remember, they aren't fully vaccinated yet, so this can be risky.

Training "Wait"

Learning to wait politely at the front door rather than bolting out is an essential skill for all dogs to master—especially large, boisterous ones. An untrained dog at the door can easily knock over visitors, injure your shoulder by pulling you out on a leash, or even run into the street and be hurt.

This command requires your dog to have reasonable impulse control, even when something exciting is happening. Be patient with your dog. Learning this skill is trickier for some pups than others, but every dog can learn polite door manners with a little time and effort.

To teach your dog to wait at the door:

Begin with your dog on-leash for safety. Stand just inside your front door.

Ask your dog to sit and say, "Wait." Reach out and lightly touch the doorknob—just a quick touch, no grasping or turning just yet. Praise and reward your dog for holding his sit.

Dog Training Commands Part II

If your dog gets excited and rushes toward the door, withhold the treat and try again. Reposition him, ask him to wait, and touch the doorknob. Praise and reward if he stays in place.

Repeat this process several times if needed. Before moving on to the next step, make sure that your dog is confidently holding his sit with no difficulty while you touch the doorknob.

Ask your dog to wait, then grasp the doorknob and start to turn it. Praise and reward if he holds his sit. If not, reposition him and try again.

Repeat step 5, and open the door just a crack. Close it again, and praise and reward your dog if he holds his sit.

Repeat, opening the door a bit wider. Work your way up to opening the door all the way, leaving it open for a moment, and then closing it again. Remember to reward your dog for staying put.

Finally, after opening the door, release your dog by saying, "Okay." Then walk through the door together.

Training "Leave It"

This is a useful command if your dog is trying to touch something that could be dangerous or if you want the dog's attention. Put a treat in both of your hands and have your hands closed. Place one hand close to your dog's face so that he can smell the treat. Then give the command *leave it*. You will find that the dog will continue to scent the treat and may even try to lick your hand. If your dog barks so to have the treat, ignore this. Just wait.

Dog Training Commands Part II

Gradually, he will lose interest. This is the moment when you offer the treat that you have in the other hand. Repeat this exercise until your dog waits patiently as soon as you utter the words, *leave it*. Then, reward with a treat.

Training "Speak"

If your dog likes to bark, this trick will likely come very naturally to him. Some dogs are quite easy to teach to bark on cue (especially vocal breeds like beagles or shelties) while others may find this skill more challenging. Either way, it's something you and your dog can have fun practicing if you want to give it a try.

To teach your dog to speak on cue:

Try getting him excited about a toy, holding a tasty treat just out of reach, or even knocking on the door—whatever works! Once you have a consistent way to prompt your dog to start barking, you're ready to begin.

Get your dog excited, then praise and reward with a treat as soon as he barks. It may take him a few repetitions to figure out what's being rewarded. Many dogs don't seem to be consciously aware that they're barking at first.

Repeat this sequence several times. You should notice that as he starts to catch on, it will take less and less prompting to get your dog to bark.

Dog Training Commands Part II

When you're sure that you can easily elicit a bark with your chosen prompt, you can introduce the verbal cue "Speak" just before you get your dog excited. Praise and reward as soon as he barks.

Try saying, "Speak," and then wait a few seconds without doing anything else. If your dog barks, praise, and reward enthusiastically. If he seems puzzled and does not bark within ten to fifteen seconds, go ahead and prompt him again with whatever you were doing before: door knocking, toy waving, or whatever it was. Repeat several more times with the prompt, then try it again with the verbal cue alone.

When your dog is confidently barking every time you say, "Speak," you can try out your new trick in other places—different parts of the house, out on a walk, etc. Visitors and people you meet outside may also enjoy asking your dog to speak.

Take It/Drop It Command

This command is useful for play purposes. The dog will drop an object as soon as you use the command or will take an object when you use the command.

Have a toy in your hand – choose a favored one and tease the dog so that he tries to take it. As soon as the dog opens his mouth, ready to take the object, give the command, *take it,* and the dog does so. Praise him. Offer another object so that the dog is tempted. As he goes to take it, he has to release the other object. Say *drop it* so that the object is released.

Dog Training Commands Part II

Then, say *take it* as he is about to take the new object. This should be repeated daily until you know that your dog has mastered this.

Chapter summary

It's essential to try and teach your pup to be as disciplined and well-behaved as possible while on a leash. A dog that pulls and bites the leash or runs away when you try to put it on is very problematic. These are warning signs that you mustn't ignore with puppies, especially if your dog is a breed that gets big.

CHAPTER 7:
Expert Social & Behavioral Training

Expert Social & Behavioral Training

Puppies have so much potential, curiosity, and intelligence. That's why puppy training begins when your puppy comes into your house — whether you want it to or not. Soiling, biting, jumping, barking, and running are natural behaviors; as a new puppy parent, it is up to you to demonstrate where and when those behaviors are appropriate and, more importantly, where they are inappropriate. Begin teaching and socializing your puppy as early as eight weeks of age if he is properly vaccinated and your veterinarian confirms his good health. Although the techniques in this chapter are best suited for puppies two to four months of age, you'll find the information valuable when training older puppies, too.

Socialization

It is crucial that you *'Socialize'* your puppy from an early age. You only have a small window of opportunity in which to do this.

A puppy should be 'Socialized' during the first 12 weeks of his life. This is the period when everything is new, and the puppy is open to new things. After this time, it may be too late, as the puppy will start to be wary of new things, and this is when unwanted behaviors can develop, e.g. barking at the vacuum cleaner.

A puppy should meet lots of people during this time, the more, the better, and make it a mix of sexes and ethnic backgrounds too if you can. Circus clowns, window cleaners, etc. get the idea?

Expert Social & Behavioral Training

Take your puppy in the car, on the bus, shopping, and walking past traffic, buses, and trucks. Use the vacuum cleaner at home and the food blender.

Once you have completed your puppy's immunizations, you can start to introduce him to other dogs and cats, and don't forget to ask people to handle him, pick him up and cuddle him.

Without this socialization, dogs can become either timid or aggressive and get very upset by a whole variety of things, from Trucks to Vacuums.

Addressing Behavioral Challenges

Young and clueless, a puppy can be a nightmare. Most puppies have behavior problems, and if you don't try to fix these early, puppies can carry these bad habits into adulthood. Puppies are like children. They need to be taught what types of behavior are acceptable and which habits are bad. This chapter will look into the most common behavior problems in puppies and how you should go about addressing them.

Excessive Barking

If your puppy barks more often than what's considered normal, there's a problem. The first step is to identify the reason behind the behavior. Excessive barking can be due to alarm, fear, boredom, loneliness, lack of attention, separation anxiety, and depression. Fortunately, there are certain ways on how you can fix this problem. It won't happen overnight, but with the proper techniques, it can be done.

Expert Social & Behavioral Training

The solution to excessive barking depends on what's causing it. If it's because of alarm and fear, you need to lessen and limit what the puppy sees. Limit the puppy's access to open windows and doors.

If the puppy spends a lot of its time in the yard or any open space, you might consider putting up a solid fence. By lessening what the puppy sees, you lessen the things that alarm it. If the excessive barking is due to boredom or loneliness, you need to provide the dog with more activities or companionship to keep him active and occupied. Buying food-dispensing toys can be an effective solution. Or you can get another puppy to be your puppy's playmate and companion.

If the excessive barking is due to a lack of attention, you have to re-train the dog. Some dogs use barking as a way to get their owner's attention. They bark if they are hungry, if they need water, if they need to go outside, etc.

It would be best if you never rewarded barking. If a dog barks and you give it food, this teaches the dog that barking means it gets what it wants. This is not good. You should stop rewarding your dog's barking antics.

If the excessive barking is due to separation anxiety, the only solution is to spend more time with your dog. It is a condition that's difficult to treat because it's a mind problem.

Expert Social & Behavioral Training

Chewing

Chewing is a normal activity for puppies, but it becomes a problem if the puppy chews on everything, including furniture and household items. The behavior can be due to puppy teething, excess energy, boredom, anxiety, and curiosity.

To fix this common problem, you must encourage your puppy to chew on the right things by giving him many chew toys. And it would help if you made the effort of keeping your personal items away from the puppy. If you have to leave your dog at home to get to work, you should also consider crating or confining the puppy in an area of the house where it can't cause damage.

If you catch your puppy chewing on something he shouldn't be chewing, correct the behavior immediately by making a sharp noise. Take away the thing and replace it with a chew toy. Do this routine every time you catch the puppy chewing on the wrong things.

Over time, the puppy will learn what to chew and what not to chew. Some dog owners recommend using bad-tasting repellants and sprays. Use these to spray on the items that you don't want the puppy to be chewing. The unpleasant taste of the repellants should help prevent the puppy from chewing on the things.

Expert Social & Behavioral Training

Digging

Most puppies do some digging, especially if they spend a good amount of their time outside, like in a yard. There are also certain breeds of dogs like Terriers prone to digging due to their hunting background.

A common cause of digging is boredom and lack of exercise. So you can fix the problem by taking your dog for a walk more often. Puppies crave activity, and if they don't get it, they resort to digging. You should also provide the dog with more toys and chews.

If you want your dog to enjoy a little bit of digging, you should designate an area in the yard where it can dig. Train the puppy to not dig in areas not covered by the designated digging area.

If you want to prohibit the puppy from digging completely, you should consider using deterrents. You discourage digging by burying the deterrents in the places where the puppy likes to dig. You can use rocks, plastic chicken wire, cayenne, vinegar, and citrus peels. If the puppy's digging habit is terrible, you can use a sprinkler with a sensor. Every time the puppy starts digging, the sensor is activated and signals the sprinkler to start raining on the puppy.

Biting and Nipping

There are several reasons why a puppy would bite a person. Dogs are possessive and can attack in an attempt to protect someone or something.

Expert Social & Behavioral Training

Fear towards people they don't know can also lead to biting. Maternal instincts and prey drive are also common causes of dog bites.

You can show your puppy that biting and nipping are not acceptable by teaching him to bite inhibition. Dog bite prevention begins at home by being a responsible dog owner. Consider neutering and spaying the puppy because this is known for decreasing biting incidents.

Solutions to biting and nipping include inhibiting, redirecting, distraction, and using deterrent products. Inhibition makes use of basic dog training methods like reinforcement. Your goal is to teach the puppy that gentle biting during play is okay, but when the biting gets harder, that's when it should stop. Redirection is a method that works in fixing mouthing, but it can also work for biting. If a puppy mouths you, you pull your hands away and then wave around a treat or a chewy toy until the puppy bites it.

Whining

A puppy whines for a variety of reasons. Maybe he needs to go potty or water, or it's hungry. Maybe he's craving for a walk in the park. These are all reasonable reasons for the puppy to whine, but sometimes the habit goes too far. That is, it whines whenever it needs something from you. You should never condone such behavior. If you give in to what the puppy wants every time it whines, you teach it to whine if it needs something.

Expert Social & Behavioral Training

To stop whining, make sure first that the puppy has no reason to whine. Make sure that he is provided with the necessities like food, water, treats, toys, and shelter.

The best strategy is not to give the puppy any attention when it whines. Pay him attention only when he goes quiet. The puppy will soon learn that whining is useless and doesn't help get the things he wants.

If the whining continues, maybe it's time to set an appointment with a vet or a dog behaviorist. It's possible that the puppy is whining because of a health problem.

Chapter summary

These are the most common behavior problems in puppies. Lack of proper socialization is the number-one reason for behavior problems. You need to expose your dog to lots of people, dogs, and environmental stimuli. Once your puppy starts displaying any of these bad habits, you should address them immediately before it gets worse or it leads to more problems. The good news is that puppies can be quick learners. With the right approach and proper training, fixing these problems shouldn't be too difficult.

Chapter 8: Puppy Loving Health Care

Puppy Loving Health Care

Raising a healthy dog is not all fun and games. You need to bring your dog to the vet for regular checkups, flea and tick control, as well as dental care. You might also want to consider neutering or spaying your dog to prevent unwanted litters from being born. Taking these steps to secure your dog's health will ensure that your dog lives a long life with you.

15 Simple Ways to care for your puppy

1. Walk your dog for 20 minutes a day. That is all it takes to extend his life by years and improve your health too.

2. Brush your dog's teeth daily and get his teeth professionally cleaned once a year if there's a lot of tartar build-up. Remember, he can't tell you if he's suffering from dental pain. To brush your dog's teeth, start slowly. Use a small toothbrush or a finger-tip brush, and always use canine toothpaste. Our toothpaste can poison a dog!

3. Take your dog for annual checkups. That doesn't mean yearly vaccinations; it's a health checkup to measure his wellbeing.

4. Keep your dog's weight low, and don't let him become part of the obesity epidemic. It's one of the biggest threats to your dog's life.

5. Reduce or cut out grains; dogs need meat, not wheat and corn. They especially don't need GMO ingredients and grist mill leftovers or sweepings.

Puppy Loving Health Care

6. Groom your dog yourself so you can check for unusual lumps, bumps, and growths. Plus, grooming can be a good bonding exercise.

7. Learn more about which vaccinations are necessary and which are dangerous. Only get the essential shots, as infrequently as possible. Remember, the push for vaccinations comes from Big Pharma and their desire to make more money.

8. Make sure you know which houseplants and garden plants are toxic for dogs and remove them.

9. Use a dog harness or kennel cage to keep your dog secure in the car. Otherwise, he's a flying missile in a sudden stop or an accident.

10. Take a pet CPR course at your local humane society.

11. If you have a small dog, avoid dog parks unless they have specific areas for dogs under 20 pounds. Even then, be very careful; the news is full of small dogs mauled to death at dog parks.

12. Make up an anti-poisoning kit and know how to use it in case your dog ingests something toxic.

13. Be sure your dog is always wearing a collar with an up-to-date tag, and consider microchipping as well. Include your phone number on the label - it's far more helpful than his name.

Puppy Loving Health Care

14. Don't feed your dog fatty meat scraps; fats can trigger pancreatitis, a painful condition. And never give him cooked bones - they shatter. Raw bones are healthy for your dog, and he'll enjoy them.

15. Spay or neuter your dog to stop diseases like cancer that attack the reproductive organs.

How to choose the right veterinarian

Before you talk to any veterinarians, ask around for recommendations from your friends, family, animal shelter, humane society, neighbors, co-workers, or breeder. As a last resort, you can try the phone book.

Once you have a list of veterinarians to speak with, come up with some questions you want to be answered before deciding on any one practitioner. Since most veterinarians are rushed (because of an overflow of clients), you may be better off, if you can afford it, to narrow down your list to 1-3 practitioners to arrange a preliminary checkup. During that meeting, you can ask any questions you want while watching the doctor handle and take care of any issues.

Appropriate medical facilities should also be sought for the dog well in advance. To make this happen this, you should hunt for a quality veterinary doctor, who may perform regular checkups and be consulted easily when your pet is undergoing any ailment. You may also consider the compatibility of your pet to the vet and not at all hesitate to arrange a meeting of the two.

Puppy Loving Health Care

The choice made should always have a scope for change. This would surely depend on the reaction of your dog and the treatment the pet is extended at their end once the visits are initiated. A few cautions which must be ensured while dealing with a veterinary set-up may be listed as follows:

* Are your queries responded to in an uncomplicated and helpful mode?

* Do you encounter any reluctance while communicating with the veterinary doctor?

* Does he pay proper attention to what you say and try to resolve your problem?

* What resources are available at the veterinary office?

* Can crisis situations be dealt with and handled with fully equipped facilities?

* Are provisions available for prompt first aid and hospitalization, if required?

* Is proper qualified staff available to look after the dog if the pet has to be admitted for a day or two?

* Is the availability of vet assured during the night hours?

* Is full co-operation being provided to you by the staff at the veterinary office?

Puppy Loving Health Care

* Are you sensing ease with the interaction between your pet and the others there?

* Do they take absolute care of your dog, or they are just business-minded intended to mint money only?

You have to keep in mind that you never hesitate to raise any query regarding your dog when you bring the pet to the vet for an examination. It helps if you can feel assured that your dog is in reliable and affectionate hands. It would prove very beneficial for you and your pet if you successfully build a fine association with an excellent veterinary clinic.

Chapter Summary

Our pets execute their best for us and we in turn should look after the basic challenges they are facing for which many times they are helpless.

Performing our duty as a good friend and master, we should educate ourselves regarding the best possible means for their health and care. Realizing that our efforts can result in raising healthy dogs, both physically and psychologically and so they can become our sincere devoted companions for years.

Conclusion

Conclusion

Thank you, and congratulations on reading until the end.

As you have seen, raising a happy, healthy, and obedient dog is not as challenging as most people think it is.

As long as you are willing to be patient with your dog as it learns, you should have no issues with completing the mission successfully.

Puppy training is a matter of your dog's wellbeing. At the same time, it's one of the most exciting and constructive ways in which you can spend time with your pet. Failing to train your pup won't just create behavioral problems and annoyances later on, but it will also deprive you of many great moments that make dog ownership so fulfilling.

Dogs are a lot like children in that all they want from you is attention and approval. As long as you manage to give out that approval selectively and appropriately, your puppy will quickly catch on and learn what they have to do to earn that approval in the future. It is why positive reinforcement and reward-based approaches work so well with dogs.

The next step is to put this information into action. You can start by teaching the puppy about the basic routines in your family so that it learns as much about its new home as possible. Proceed to teach some basic obedience commands like come, stay, sit, etc. These form the basis of all the other commands you will teach.

Conclusion

Always have treats and toys on hand when you're teaching commands. These are meant to condition the puppy to associate the cues with goodies.

Continue teaching the puppy the other commands while exposing it to the environment in which it will live to help build its social skills. Don't get tired of repeating a command. Your puppy won't grasp everything in one session or the first week, but this doesn't mean that you should give up. Keep going until the dog grasps everything.

Lastly, it is essential to remember that dog training is a long-term, ongoing process that doesn't necessarily have to stop at a certain point. Just because you've taught your pup to fetch and walk at your heel doesn't mean you should stop there. Like people, dogs can learn as long as they live, and it's never a bad time to try and teach your dog a new trick or two, even if he is getting older. In the end, your pet will be grateful for the attention and commitment that you have given.

If you found the book valuable, can you recommend it to others? One way to do that is to post a review on Amazon.

Thank you, and much success!

Book Title:

We want to thank you for the purchase of this book and more importantly, thank you for reading it to the end. We hope your reading experience was pleasurable and that you would inform your family and friends on Facebook, Twitter or other social media.

We would like to continue to provide you with high-quality books, and that end, would you mind leaving us a review on Amazon.com?

Just use the link below, scroll down about 3/4 of the page and you will see images similar to the one below.

We are extremely grateful for your assistance.

Warm Regards, MahoneyProducts Publishing

Book Link:
https://www.amazon.com/dp/B095GLRYNP

Customer reviews

4.6 out of 5 stars

4.6 out of 5
6 global ratings

5 star	64%
4 star	36%-
3 star 0% (0%)	0%
2 star 0% (0%)	0%
1 star 0% (0%)	

Review this product

Share your thoughts with other customers

(Write a Customer Review)

You might also enjoy:

Starting a Dog Breeding Business
Step by Step How to Get Money, Supplies & Equipment

By Brian Mahoney

Imagine you can have the knowledge you want to start your business and live the Hassle Free All-American Lifestyle of Independence, Prosperity and Peace of Mind. Discover how to....

* Discover from this book step by step how to start your business

* A guide for quick & easy access to wholesale Dog Breeding & dog training supplies

* Learn how to write a Business Plan for your Dog Breeding business

* The benefits of Business Insurance

* Get Colossal Free Cash from Crowdfunding

* How to Get access to a Goldmine of Government Grants

* How to Market to a Billion People for FREE!

* Dog Breeding & Dog Breeds Web Resource Guide for quick access to training & certification

and Much Much More!

You have the right to restore a culture of the can-do spirit and enjoy the financial security you and your family deserve. People are destroyed for lack of knowledge. Get the knowledge you need to start living your business dreams!

Don't wait. You'll wait your life away...

Amazon.com Book Link:
https://www.amazon.com/dp/1951929136

Leave a review and join Our VIP Mailing List Then Get All our Audio Books Free! We will be releasing a ton money making & self help audio books within the next 12 months! Just leave a review and join our mailing list and get them all for free!

Just Hit/Type in the Link Below

https://urlzs.com/HfbGF

www.ingramcontent.com/pod-product-compliance
Lightning Source LLC
Chambersburg PA
CBHW052113110526
44592CB00013B/1587